A Use the words in the box to write a sentence using *commas*.

run	skip	jump

On Sports Day _____

_____

_____

B Write sentences with a list of:

Don't forget to use **commas**!

1 your favourite food

_____

_____

2 your favourite lessons

_____

_____

3 your favourite animals

_____

_____

Support

A Underline the *adjectives*.
Circle the *comparative adjectives*.

1 The people waited on the crowded platform.

2 The train was late.

3 "It was later than this yesterday," said one man.

4 "We need a faster train," said another.

5 "Even if the train is late, it is quicker than walking," said the stationmaster.

B Complete the table.

Add **er** to the adjective.

adjective	comparative adjective
soft	
strong	
great	
sharp	
old	
bright	

To make **comparative adjectives** that:

- have one **syllable** and end in **vowel – consonant** = **double** the last letter + **er**

> Look at these **comparative adjectives.**

  b**ig**   bi**gg**er   fla**t**   fla**tt**er

- end in **e** = just add **r**

  wid**e**   wide**r**   larg**e**   large**r**

- end in **y** = change the **y** to **i** and add **er**

  happ**y**   happ**ier**   prett**y**   prett**ier**

Follow the rules and complete the table.

adjective	comparative adjective	adjective	comparative adjective
cloudy		simple	
brave		squeaky	
safe		late	
lovely		tasty	
ripe		sleepy	

Support

The first one is done for you.

A Match.

the shoes belonging to the boy   Mum's umbrella

the growl belonging to the tiger   the man's dog

the dog belonging to the man   the boy's shoes

the umbrella belonging to Mum   the farmer's boots

the boots belonging to the farmer   the tiger's growl

B Underline the *owner* in each sentence.

1 the elephant's trunk   2 the bird's feathers

3 the zebra's stripes   4 the bee's buzz

5 the dog's paw   6 the rabbit's ears

C Add the missing apostrophes.

Look for the owner!

1 Sams ball is in the pond.

2 The girls coat is wet.

3 A snakes skin is cold.

Extension

A Add the missing *apostrophes*.

1 Michaels feet were sore after the race.

2 That bakers bread is the best in town.

3 My friends sister is three today.

4 The trees branches swayed in the wind.

5 The cars tyres were stuck in the mud.

B Write each phrase in a shorter way using a *possessive apostrophe*. Use each one in a sentence of your own.

1 the rays belonging to the sun _____

Sentence: _____

_____

2 the bike belonging to the postman _____

Sentence: _____

_____

3 the roar belonging to the lion _____

Sentence: _____

_____

4 the letter belonging to the girl _____

Sentence: _____

_____

Support

The first one is done for you.

A Match the words and their *contractions*.

is not	doesn't
are not	wouldn't
must not	weren't
do not	isn't
does not	wasn't
cannot	mustn't
would not	shouldn't
have not	can't
was not	aren't
were not	hasn't
has not	haven't
should not	don't

B Use these *contractions* in sentences of your own.

1 doesn't _____

_____

2 wasn't _____

_____

3 can't _____

_____

Extension

Write the *contraction*. Use it in a sentence.

1 we shall   contraction _____

Sentence: _____

_____

2 let us   contraction _____

Sentence: _____

_____

3 that is   contraction _____

Sentence: _____

_____

4 there is   contraction _____

Sentence: _____

_____

5 who has   contraction _____

Sentence: _____

_____

Support

A Underline the *past tense verbs*.

1 The dog was barking loudly.

2 The shopkeeper was closing the shop.

3 Dad was making tea.

4 The builder was mending the wall.

5 Our friends were coming to see us.

The first one
is done for you.

B Finish the table.

present simple tense	past simple tense	past progressive tense
I walk	I walked	I was walking
They save		
We talk		
You jump		
He smiles		
It barks		

Extension

A Complete the sentence.
Add a *past progressive verb* to each sentence.

The **verb family name** will help you.

1 (to post)

Jill _____ _____ a letter when she saw her friend.

2 (to talk)

The children _____ _____ until the teacher came in.

3 (to go)

I _____ _____ to cut the grass but it started to rain.

4 (to watch)

We had a power cut while we _____ _____ television.

B Write sentences in the *past tense* which have these pairs of actions.

The first one is done for you.

1 action 1: was carrying   action 2: snapped

I was carrying the bag when the handle snapped.

2 action 1: were watching   action 2: knocked

_____

_____

3 action 1: was running   action 2: arrived

_____

_____

Support

A Underline the *adjectives*.
Circle the *superlative adjectives*.

1 We are going to put up our new tent.

2 We need to find the smoothest spot
to put it on.

3 Use the strongest rope you can find.

4 Did we have to choose the coldest day?

5 We will soon be inside our warm tent.

> Add **est** to
> the adjective.

B Complete the table.

adjective	superlative adjective
soft	
strong	
great	
sharp	
old	
bright	

Extension

To make **superlative adjectives** that:

- have **one syllable** and end in **vowel – consonant** = **double** the last letter + **est**

    bi**g**   bigg**est**   fla**t**   flatt**est**

- end in **e** = just add **st**

    wide   wide**st**   large   large**st**

- end in **y** = change the **y** to **i** and add **er**

    happy   happ**ier**   pretty   prett**ier**

> Look at these **superlative adjectives**.

Follow the rules and complete the table.

adjective	superlative adjective
cloudy	
brave	
safe	
lovely	
ripe	
simple	
squeaky	
later	
tasty	
sleepy	

Support

A Underline the *adverb* in each sentence.

1 She wrote the letter carefully.

2 I never eat prawns.

3 We are going to the cinema tonight.

4 I hid behind the tree.

5 He stayed indoors when it snowed.

B Finish these sentences with *adverbs* of your own.

How adverbs

1 The dog barked _____.

2 The owl hooted _____.

When adverbs

1 It is sunny _____.

2 I _____ go swimming.

Where adverbs

1 The horse jumped _____ the fence.

2 The dog lives _____ a kennel.

Extension

The first one is done for you.

A Build sentences.
Add an *adjective* (**1**) and an *adverb* (**2**) to each sentence to make it more interesting.

1 The (1) _____tall_____ tree swayed (2) __dangerously__ .

2 She sweeps the (1) _____ floor (2) _____ .

3 The (1) _____ elephant charged (2) _____ .

B Write an *adverb*. Use it in a *sentence*.

1 **How adverb** _____

Sentence: _____

_____

2 **When adverb** _____

Sentence: _____

_____

3 **Where adverb** _____

Sentence: _____

_____

15

Support

A Write each *verb* under the correct heading.

was finding	carried	were shopping	pointed
waved	was raining	was sleeping	cheered
were searching	liked	was crying	shared

past simple tense	past progressive tense

B Add a *past progressive verb* to each sentence.

> The verb family name will help you.

1 (to water)

I _____ _____ the plants when my friend knocked on the door.

2 (to wait)

She _____ _____ at the station when the train arrived.

3 (to dig)

He _____ _____ the garden when the spade broke.

Extension

The first one is done for you.

Write sentences in the *past tense* which have these pairs of actions.

1 action 1: was drawing   action 2: snapped

I was drawing a picture when my pencil snapped.

2 action 1: were swimming   action 2: appeared

_____

_____

3 action 1: were working   action 2: arrived

_____

_____

4 action 1: was raining   action 2: flashed

_____

_____

5 action 1: were escaping   action 2: stopped

_____

_____

Conjunctions

Join these pairs of sentences with *and*, *but* or *or*. The first one is done for you.

1   I had a map.
    I got lost.
    <u>I had a map but I got lost.</u>

You need **one** capital letter and **one** full stop.

2   I think I will phone my friend.
    I might text her.

    _____

    _____

3   The concert was great.
    I enjoyed myself.

    _____

    _____

4   We could buy him a jumper.
    We could buy him a tie.

    _____

    _____

Extension

A Write two *sentences* about this picture.

_____

_____

_____

Join the two sentences with *but*.

_____

_____

B Write two *questions* about this picture.

_____

_____

_____

Join the two sentences with *or*.

_____

_____

Support

A Write *two*, *too* or *to* in each gap.

1 _____ and _____ make four.

$$2+2=4$$

2 There are _____ many flowers in this vase.

3 Go _____ and read your book.

4 I would like some cake, _____.

B Write sentences.

1 Write a sentence using **two**.

_____

_____

2 Write a sentence using **too**.

_____

_____

3 Write a sentence using **to**.

_____

_____

Extension

there = about **place**.

The cinema is over **there**.

their = **belonging to them**

They got **their** coats dirty.

they're = **they are**

They're very late!

These words can be confusing.

A Use *there*, *their* or *they're* to fill each gap.

1 I think we catch the bus over _____.

2 Where did you find _____ hats?

3 Max went to his friends' house and played with _____ dog.

4 I think _____ riding _____ bikes.

5 _____ going to buy _____ car from the garage over _____.

B Write a sentence using all three words.

there	their	they're

_____

_____

_____

Conjunctions

A Underline the *conjunction* in each sentence.

1   We left the city and moved to a village.

2   We wanted to live in a village because
we like the countryside.

3   We bought a house next to a field so we could have a horse.

4   We have a big garden because Mum likes gardening.

B Join each pair of sentences with a *conjunction* from the box.

so	but	because

1   There is a church in the village.
There is no shop in the village.

_____

_____

2   We bought bicycles.
We can ride to school.

_____

_____

3   Dad is digging a vegetable patch.
We want to grow vegetables.

_____

_____

Extension

A Join each pair of sentences using *but*, *so* or *because*. Change the underlined words to *pronouns*.

1 Ella wanted her tea early.
<u>Ella</u> could meet her friends.

_____

_____

2 Tom wanted to wear boots.
<u>Tom</u> could not find them.

_____

_____

3 The snake rested under a rock.
<u>The snake</u> was hot.

_____

_____

B Write sentences that use each of these *conjunctions*.

1 and _____

_____

2 but _____

_____

3 so _____

_____

4 because _____

_____

Support

A Complete the table. The first one has been done for you.

adverb	comparative	superlative
late	later	latest
fast		
high		
near		
hard		

B Underline the *comparative* and *superlative* adverbs in these sentences.

1 He jumped the highest and won the competition.

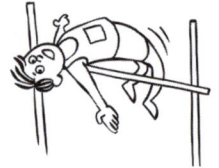

2 I moved nearer so I could see more.

3 If you work harder, you will get it right.

4 I got home later than usual.

5 She finished faster than anyone else.

C Use these *adverbs* in sentences of your own.

1 higher _____

_____

2 fast _____

_____

Extension

These are tricky.

adverb	comparative	superlative
well	better	best
badly	worse	worst
little	less	least
much	more	most
far	further	furthest

A Fill in the missing *adverbs*.

1 I did well in the test but Sam did _____.

2 Amy walked far but Lisa walked _____.

3 I ate little but my friend ate _____.

4 I scored badly in the class in my spelling test but my friend scored the _____.

The first one is done for you.

B *Adverb* or *adjective*? Tick the right column.

	adverb	adjective
1 The dog ran <u>fast</u>.	✓	
2 I enjoyed that <u>late</u> television programme.		
3 The rocket flew <u>high</u> into the clouds.		
4 The <u>high</u> building was amazing.		
5 The <u>nearest</u> book is the one you want.		
6 The <u>fast</u> car was speeding.		
7 The cat crawled <u>nearer</u> to the bird.		
8 I will go to the shops <u>later</u>.		

UNIT 27 Nouns

Support

A Make *nouns* from these verbs by adding *er*.

verb			noun
1 walk	+	er =	_____
2 build	+	er =	_____
3 garden	+	er =	_____
4 sing	+	er =	_____
5 clean	+	er =	_____

Watch your spelling!

B Make *nouns* from these verbs by adding *ing*.

verb			noun
1 drive	+	ing =	_____
2 act	+	ing =	_____
3 bake	+	ing =	_____
4 fish	+	ing =	_____
5 iron	+	ing =	_____

Extension

adjective				noun	
happy	+	**ness**	=	happ**iness**	
lazy	+	**ness**	=	laz**iness**	
tidy	+	**ness**	=	tid**iness**	

Look at these **nouns**.

A Follow the rule. Write the *nouns*.

1 ugly   +   ness = _____

2 lonely +   ness = _____

3 pretty +   ness = _____

4 lovely +   ness = _____

5 foggy +   ness = _____

B Choose three of the *nouns* you have made in **A**. Use each *noun* in a sentence of your own.

1 _____

_____

2 _____

_____

3 _____

_____

Support

A Make the words in the box into *adjectives*.
Write them under the correct heading.

| home | price | help | truth | worth | play | end | peace |

+ ful	+ less

B Use these *adjectives* in sentences of your own.

1 useless _____

_____

2 priceless _____

_____

3 homeless _____

_____

4 peaceful _____

_____

Extension

beauty + ful = beauti**ful**

Look at these **adjectives**.

penny + less = penni**less**

A Complete each sentence with a *'ful' adjective*.

1 If you do your duty, you are _____.

2 If you show mercy, you are _____.

3 If there is plenty of something, it is _____.

B Use each of the *adjectives* you have made in **A** in sentences of your own.

1 _____

_____

2 _____

_____

3 _____

_____

Pronouns

Fill each gap with a *pronoun*.

1 Ian felt sick because _____ had eaten too much.
2 If Tina wanted to, _____ could play outside.
3 Aunt Mary was cross with the dog because _____ had chewed the rug.

Contractions

Write the *contractions*.

1 she has _____

2 we have _____

3 it has _____

4 they have _____

Commas

Fill in the missing *commas*.

1 I can see a bird a tree and a nest.
2 She needs flour eggs butter and water for the cake.
3 Sally Ben Jim Amy Tom and I are making a den.

Nouns

Write the *collective nouns*.

1 an _____ of soldiers

2 a _____ of flowers

3 a _____ of books

4 a _____ of geese